dedication

I dedicate this book to the past, present and future students of The Creative Edge at ASHMCC Online Art School. May you be liberated to create endlessly from the soul.

the **rights**

Copyright © 2023
Ashley Mullen Creative Consulting, LLC

table of contents

5	introduction
7	essential materials
11	bushes + uses
15	layering + blending technique
19	basic elements of art
23	color theory
27	abstract approaches
31	color schemes
35	composition
39	value + depth
43	color + mood
47	the influencers
52	resources
53	about the author

introduction

Welcome to this glossary of terms for acrylic painting!

Whether you're a beginner or an experienced painter, this guide is designed to help you navigate the world of acrylics with ease.

Acrylic painting is a versatile and exciting medium, but it can also be intimidating if you're not familiar with the terminology. This glossary aims to demystify the jargon and provide clear, concise definitions of the key terms and techniques you'll encounter when working with acrylics.

From basic terms like "canvas" and "brush" to more advanced concepts like "underpainting" and "glazing," this guide will equip you with the knowledge you need to confidently tackle any acrylic painting project.

So, whether you're looking to expand your vocabulary, refine your technique, or simply deepen your appreciation for this wonderful medium, this glossary is the perfect place to start.

Let's dive in!

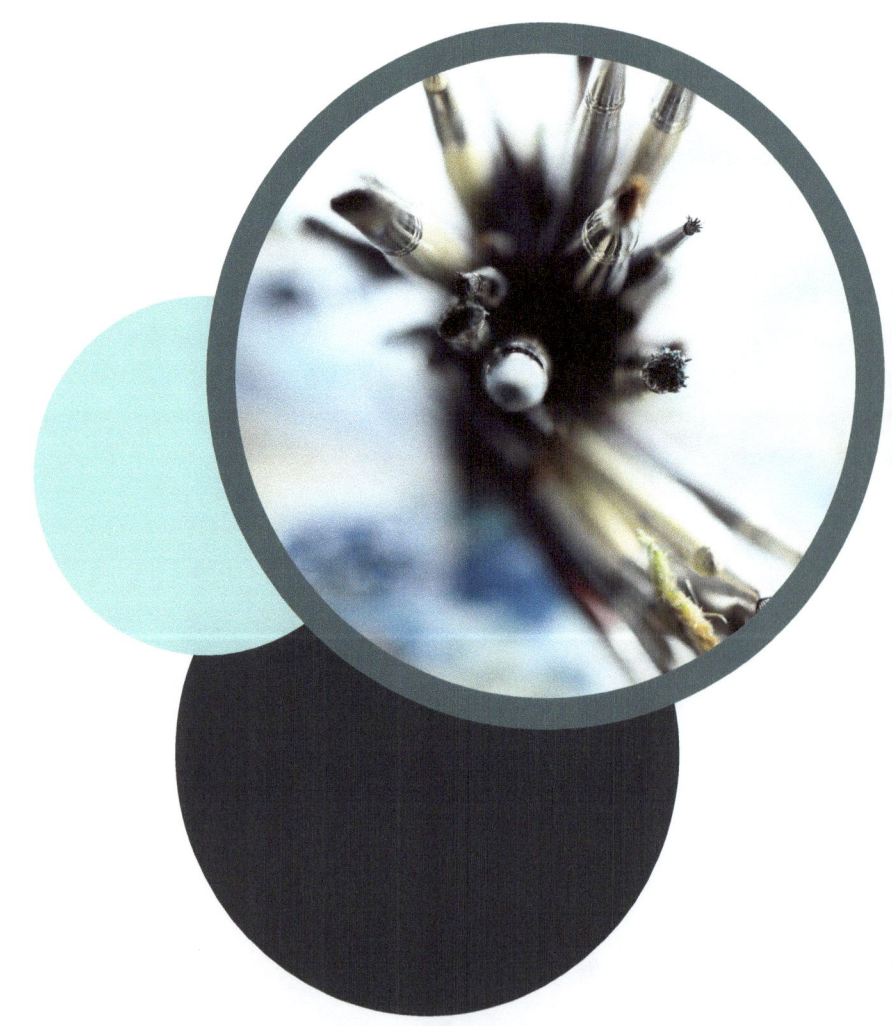

essential materials

Acrylic Paint
Acrylic paint is a fast-drying water-based paint that consists of pigments suspended in an acrylic polymer emulsion. It comes in a wide range of colors and can be used to create a variety of effects, from opaque to translucent to transparent.

Paintbrushes
Paintbrushes are used to apply acrylic paint to a surface. There are many different types of paintbrushes, including flat, round, filbert, and fan brushes, each with its own unique shape and texture.

Painting Surface
The painting surface is the material on which the acrylic paint is applied. Popular options include canvas, paper, wood, and acrylic panels.

Palette
A palette is used to hold and mix acrylic paint. It can be made of plastic, glass, or wood and comes in various shapes and sizes.

Palette Knife
A palette knife is a tool with a flexible blade that is used to mix paint on the palette and apply it to the painting surface. It can also be used to create texture and scrape away excess paint.

Water
Water is used to thin acrylic paint and clean brushes.

Mediums
Mediums are additives that can be mixed with acrylic paint to alter its properties. For example, a gloss medium can be used to create a shiny surface, while a texture medium can be used to create texture.

Gesso
Gesso is a primer that is applied to the painting surface to create a smooth, even surface for the acrylic paint. It can also be used to create texture.

Easel
An easel is a stand that holds the painting surface in a vertical position, making it easier to paint.

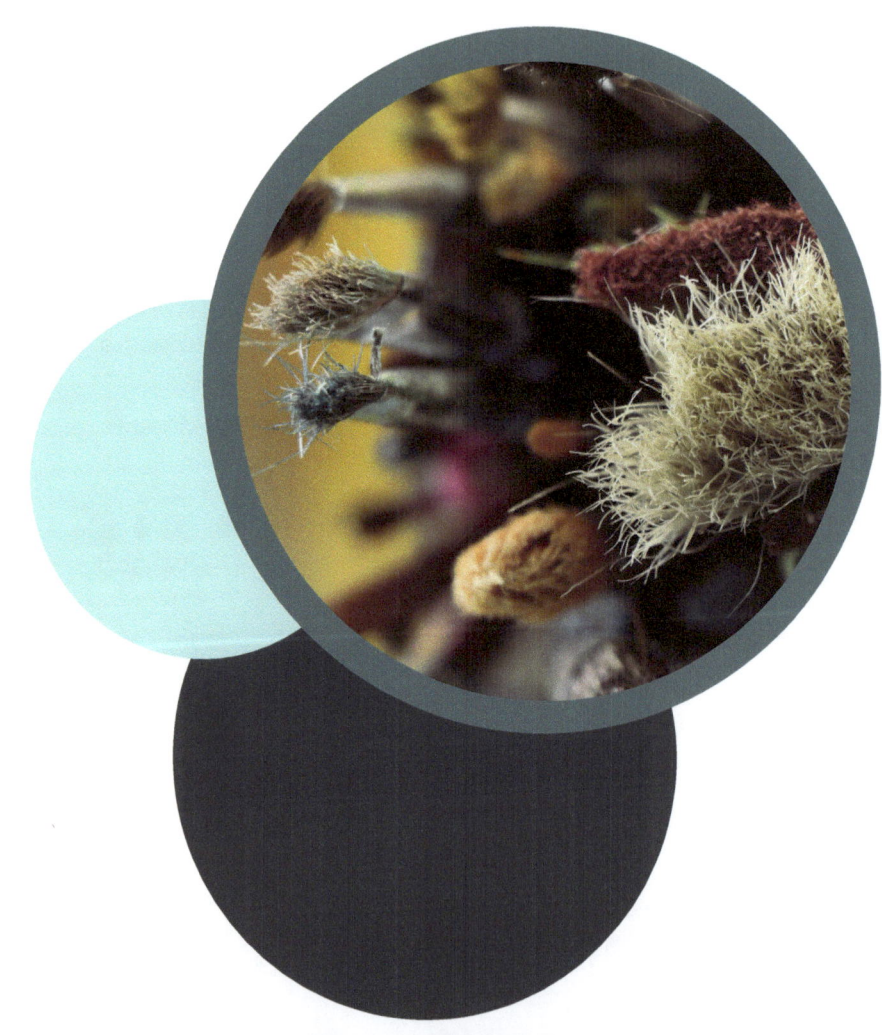

brushes +uses

Flat brushes
These have a flat shape and are great for creating clean, straight strokes and for painting large areas. They come in a variety of sizes, and larger flat brushes are often used for covering large areas with a base color or background.

Round brushes
These have a pointed tip and are great for creating fine details, lines, and curves. They come in a variety of sizes, and smaller round brushes are often used for intricate details and highlights.

Filbert brushes
These have a flat, oval-shaped tip, making them a great all-purpose brush for blending, creating rounded edges, and creating soft, gradual transitions. They are often used for painting foliage, clouds, and other organic shapes.

Fan brushes
These have a flat, fan-shaped tip, and are great for creating texture, blending, and softening edges. They are often used for painting grass, foliage, and other natural textures.

Angular brushes
These have a angled tip, making them great for creating sharp lines, edges, and corners. They are often used for painting architectural details, lettering, and geometric shapes.

Mop brushes
These have a large, round shape and are great for creating soft, blended areas, and for adding a wash of color to a large area. They are often used for painting skies and large backgrounds.

Detail brushes
These have a very fine, pointed tip and are great for creating tiny details and precise lines. They are often used for painting small details such as eyelashes, flowers, and lettering.

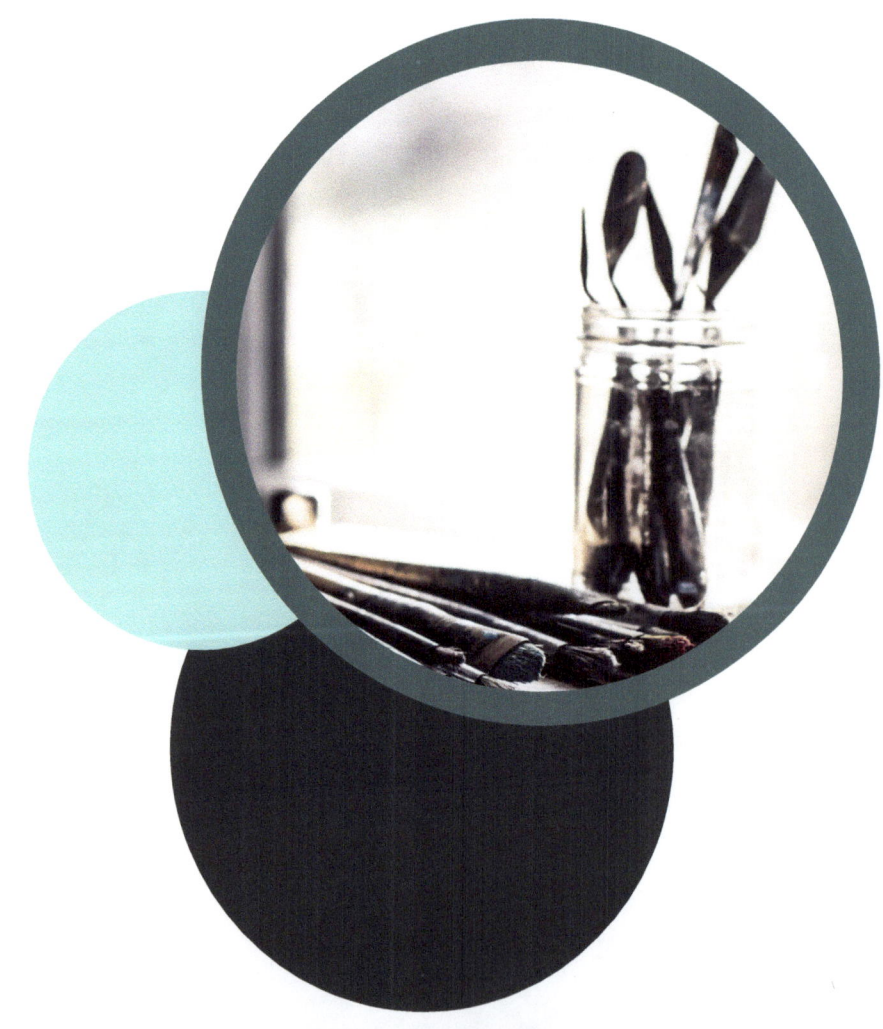

layering+ blending **technique**

Glazing
Glazing involves applying thin layers of transparent or translucent paint over previously dried layers. This technique is often used to create depth and luminosity in a painting.

Scumbling
Scumbling involves applying dry brushstrokes of color over a dry base layer. This technique is often used to create a textured, broken effect.

Wet-on-wet
Wet-on-wet involves applying wet paint onto a wet surface. This technique is often used to create soft blends and transitions between colors.

Dry Brushing
Dry brushing involves using a brush with very little paint to create a textured, scratchy effect. This technique is often used to create highlights and details.

Impasto
Impasto involves applying thick layers of paint with a palette knife or brush. This technique is often used to create texture and three-dimensional effects.

Sgraffito
Sgraffito involves scratching or scraping away layers of paint to reveal the layers underneath. This technique is often used to create texture and highlights.

Gradient
Gradient involves blending two or more colors to create a smooth transition from one color to another. This technique is often used to create smooth, continuous transitions between colors.

Layering
Layering involves applying multiple layers of paint over each other to create depth and texture. This technique is often used to build up the surface of a painting and create a sense of depth.

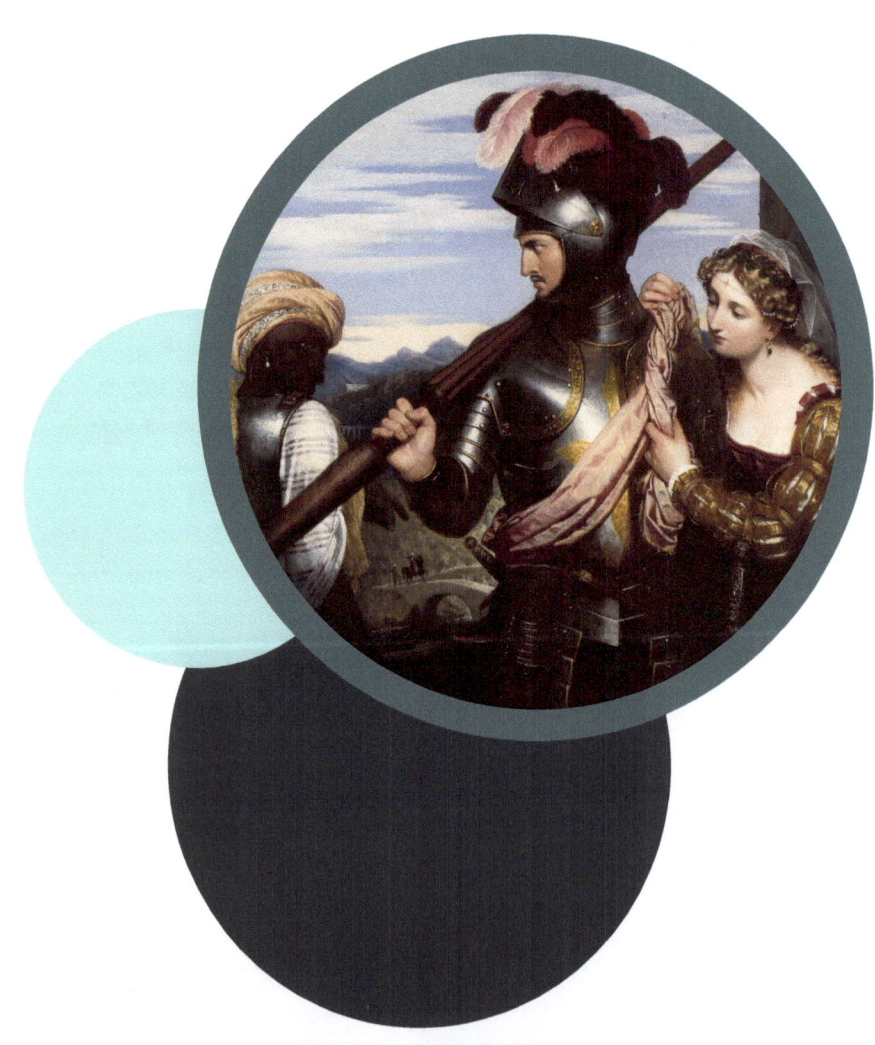

basic elements **of art**

Brushwork
The marks made by a brush, often used to create texture, movement, or pattern in an acrylic painting.

Color mixing
The process of combining two or more colors to create a new color or shade, often used to create depth and variation in an acrylic painting.

Underpainting
A layer of paint applied to a canvas or surface before the final layers, often used to create a foundation of color and value in an acrylic painting.

Wash
A thin layer of paint or watercolor applied to a surface, often used to create a transparent or translucent effect in an acrylic painting.

Medium
A substance added to acrylic paint to alter its texture, transparency, or drying time, often used to create unique effects and finishes in an acrylic painting.

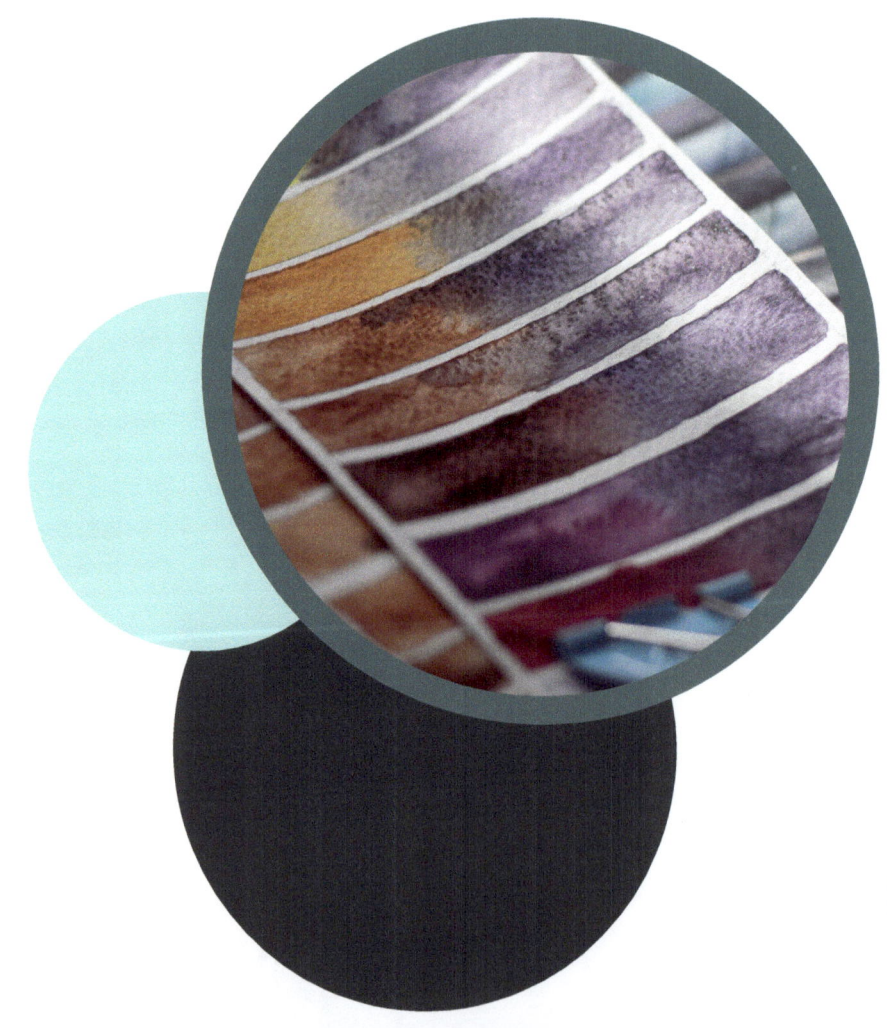

color **theory**

Hue
The property that distinguishes one color from another, such as red, blue, or yellow.

Value
The relative lightness or darkness of a color.

Saturation
The purity or intensity of a color.

Primary Colors
The three colors (red, blue, and yellow) from which all other colors can be created.

Secondary Colors
The three colors (green, orange, and purple) created by mixing two primary colors together.

Tertiary Colors
The six colors created by mixing a primary color with a secondary color.

Complementary Colors
Colors that are opposite each other on the color wheel, such as red and green or blue and orange.

Analogous Colors
Colors that are adjacent to each other on the color wheel, such as yellow, yellow-green, and green.

Monochromatic Colors
Different shades and tints of a single color.

Warm Color
Colors that are associated with warmth and energy, such as reds, oranges, and yellows.

Cool Colors
Colors that are associated with calm and relaxation, such as blues, greens, and purples.

Color Harmony
The use of different colors in a way that is aesthetically pleasing and creates a sense of balance in a painting.

Color Contrast
The use of colors that differ in hue, value, or saturation to create visual interest and emphasize certain elements in a painting.

Color Temperature
The perceived warmth or coolness of a color.

Color Wheel
A circular diagram used to organize colors and demonstrate color relationships.

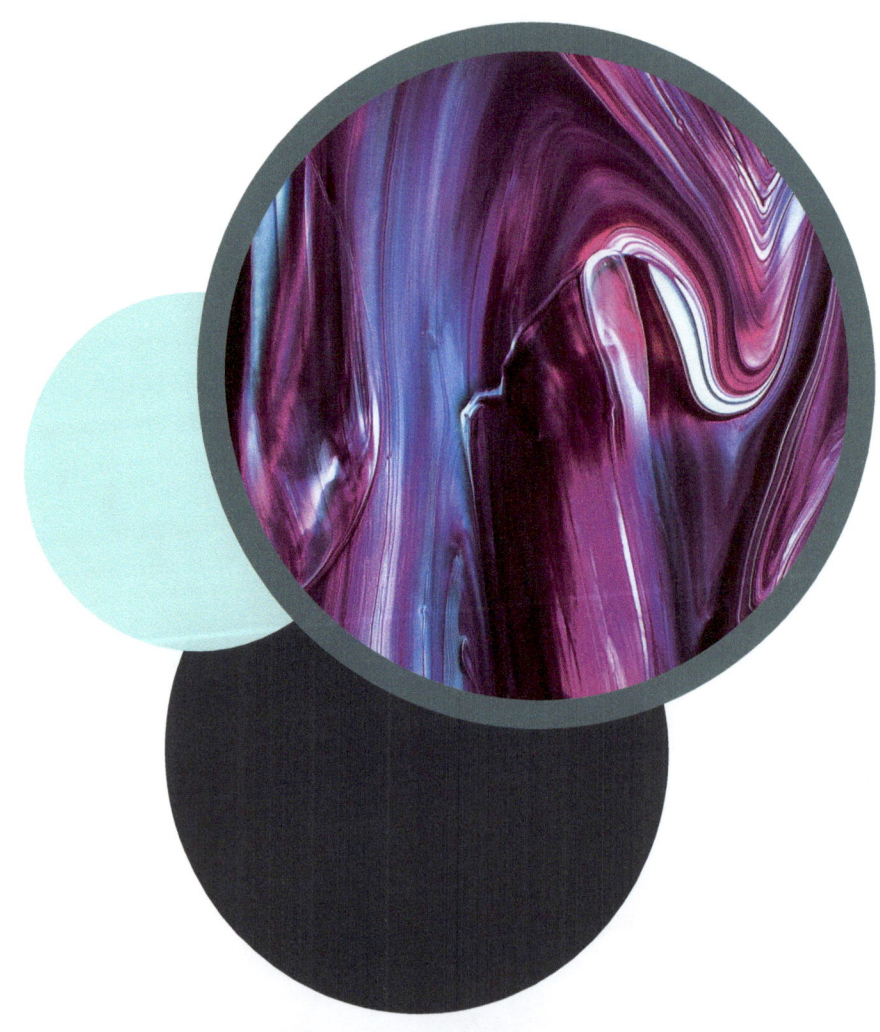

abstract **approaches**

Dripping
A technique developed by Jackson Pollock in which paint is dripped or poured onto a canvas or other surface, often using a stick or brush. The resulting marks and splatters create a sense of movement and energy in the painting.

Layering
A technique in which multiple layers of paint are applied to a surface, often using a variety of tools and techniques. This can create a sense of depth and texture in the painting, as well as build up a complex visual language.

Pouring
A technique in which paint is mixed with a pouring medium, such as a resin or varnish, and then poured onto a surface. The resulting forms and shapes are often unpredictable and create a sense of organic movement in the painting.

Color field painting
A style of abstract painting that emphasizes large fields of color, often with little or no discernible brushstrokes or other marks. This approach often creates a sense of calmness and contemplation in the viewer.

Action painting
A style of abstract painting that emphasizes the physical act of painting, often using gestural brushstrokes, dripping, and other techniques to create a sense of movement and energy.

Abstraction in nature
A style of abstract painting that takes inspiration from natural forms and shapes, such as landscapes or geological formations, and distills them into abstracted shapes and colors.

Geometric abstraction
A style of abstract painting that emphasizes geometric shapes, such as squares, circles, and triangles, often arranged in precise patterns or grids. This approach often creates a sense of order and balance in the painting.

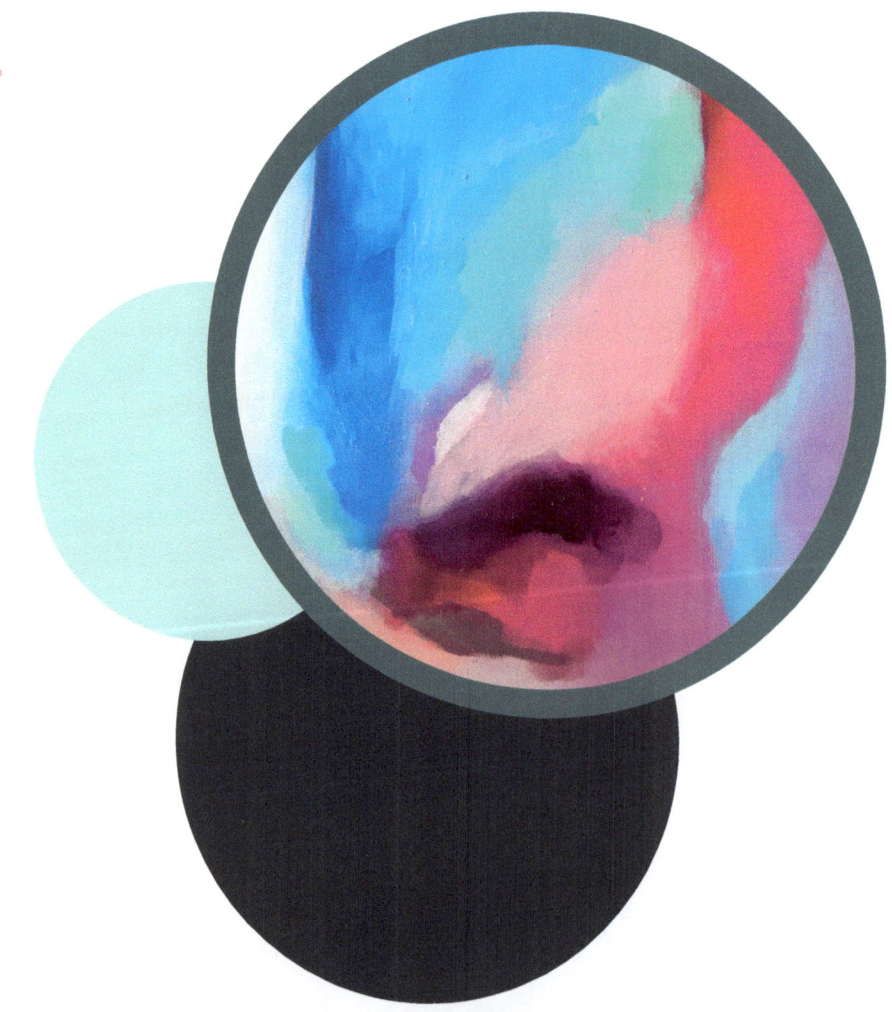

color**schemes**

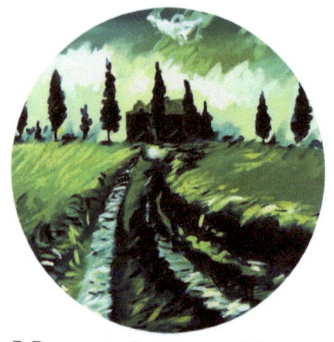 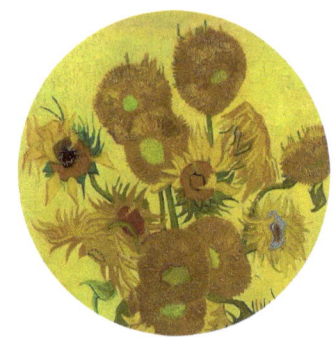

Monochromatic

A monochromatic color scheme involves using a single color in varying shades, tints, and tones. This creates a harmonious and cohesive painting with a single dominant color.

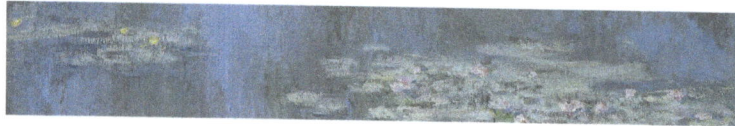

Analogous

An analogous color scheme involves using colors that are adjacent to each other on the color wheel, such as blue, green, and yellow-green. This creates a painting with a sense of harmony and unity, as the colors are closely related.

Complimentary

A complimentary color scheme involves using colors that are opposite each other on the color wheel, such as blue and orange or red and green. This creates a painting with a sense of contrast and tension, as the colors are opposing forces.

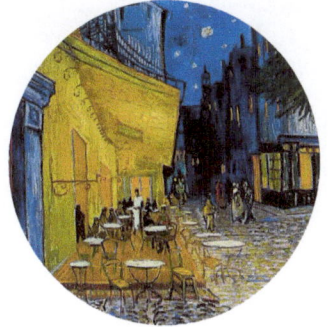 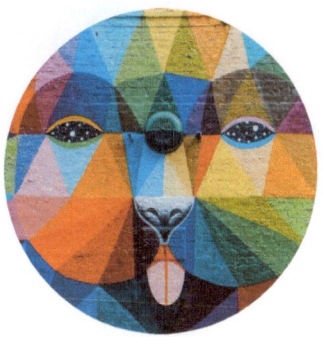

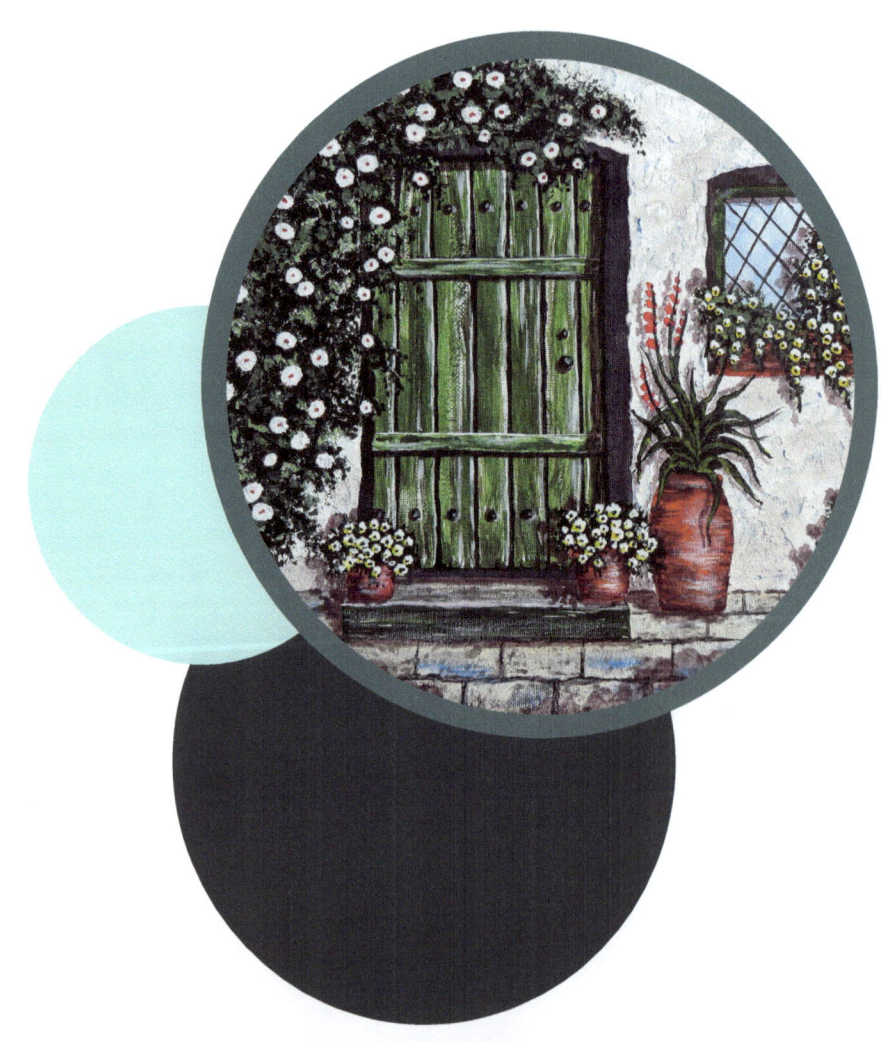

composition

Composition
The arrangement of elements within a painting, including the placement of objects, shapes, colors, and values.

Balance
The distribution of visual weight in a painting, which can be achieved through symmetrical, asymmetrical, or radial balance.

Focal point
The area of a painting that draws the viewer's eye and is usually the most important element in the composition.

Rule of thirds
A guideline for composition that suggests dividing the painting into thirds both horizontally and vertically, and placing the focal point at one of the intersections of those lines.

Negative space
The area around the objects in a painting, which can be used to create balance and contrast.

Repetition
The use of similar elements, such as shapes, colors, or values, throughout a painting to create unity and harmony.

Contrast
The difference between light and dark values, or between different colors or textures, which can create visual interest and draw the viewer's eye.

Scale
The relative size of objects within a painting, which can be used to create a sense of depth and distance.

Rhythm
The repetition of patterns, lines, shapes, or colors throughout a painting, which can create a sense of movement and visual interest.

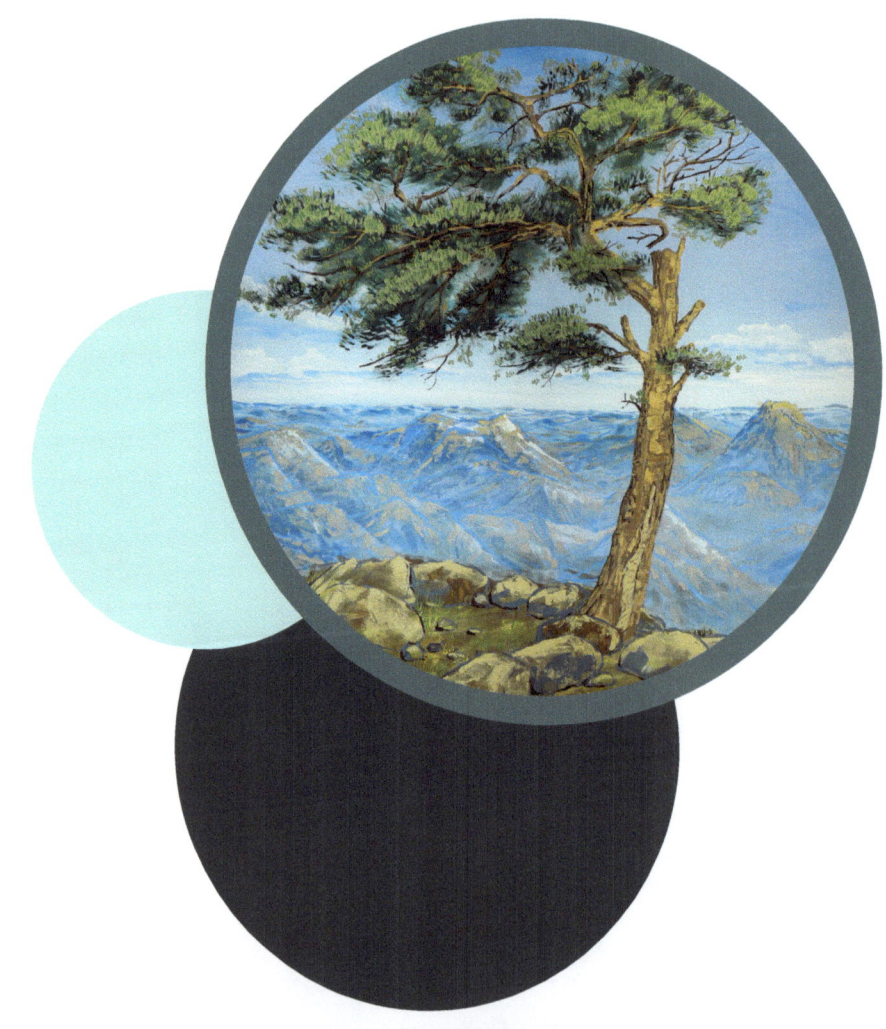

value+**depth**

Atmospheric Perspective
This refers to the natural effect of the atmosphere on the appearance of objects as they recede into the distance. As objects move farther away, they appear lighter in value and less detailed. Artists can create this effect in their paintings by gradually lightening the value of objects as they move into the distance.

Shading
The use of light and shadow can create the appearance of depth in a painting. By using lighter values on areas that receive more light and darker values on areas that receive less light, artists can create the illusion of three-dimensional form and depth.

Highlight and Shadow
By adding highlights (the lightest value) and shadows (the darkest value) to an object, artists can create the illusion of depth and form. The highlight and shadow can be used to emphasize the curvature of an object, creating the illusion of a three-dimensional form.

Contrast
Contrast refers to the difference in value between different areas of a painting. By creating strong contrasts between the light and dark areas of a painting, artists can create a sense of depth and make objects appear more three-dimensional.

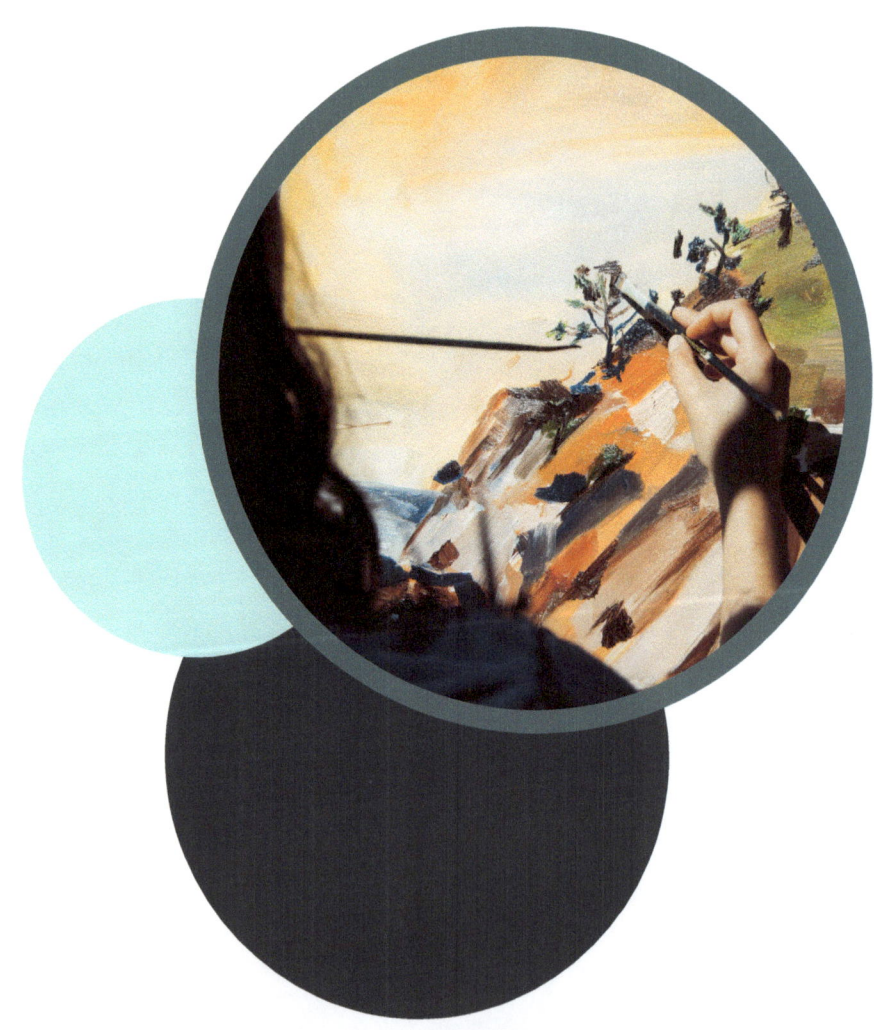

color+mood

Warm and cool colors
Warm colors, such as reds, oranges, and yellows, tend to evoke feelings of energy and excitement, while cool colors, such as blues, greens, and purples, tend to create a sense of calm and relaxation.

Bright and muted colors
Bright, saturated colors can create a sense of joy and playfulness, while muted or desaturated colors can convey a sense of sadness or melancholy.

Complementary colors
The use of complementary colors, such as red and green or blue and orange, can create a sense of tension or contrast in a painting, which can be used to evoke a particular emotion.

Color temperature
The perceived warmth or coolness of a color can also affect mood. Warm colors tend to create a sense of comfort and intimacy, while cool colors can be used to create a sense of detachment or isolation.

Color symbolism
Certain colors are often associated with specific emotions or ideas, such as red with passion or anger, blue with sadness or calmness, and green with nature or growth. Artists can use these associations to create a specific mood or convey a particular message in their paintings.

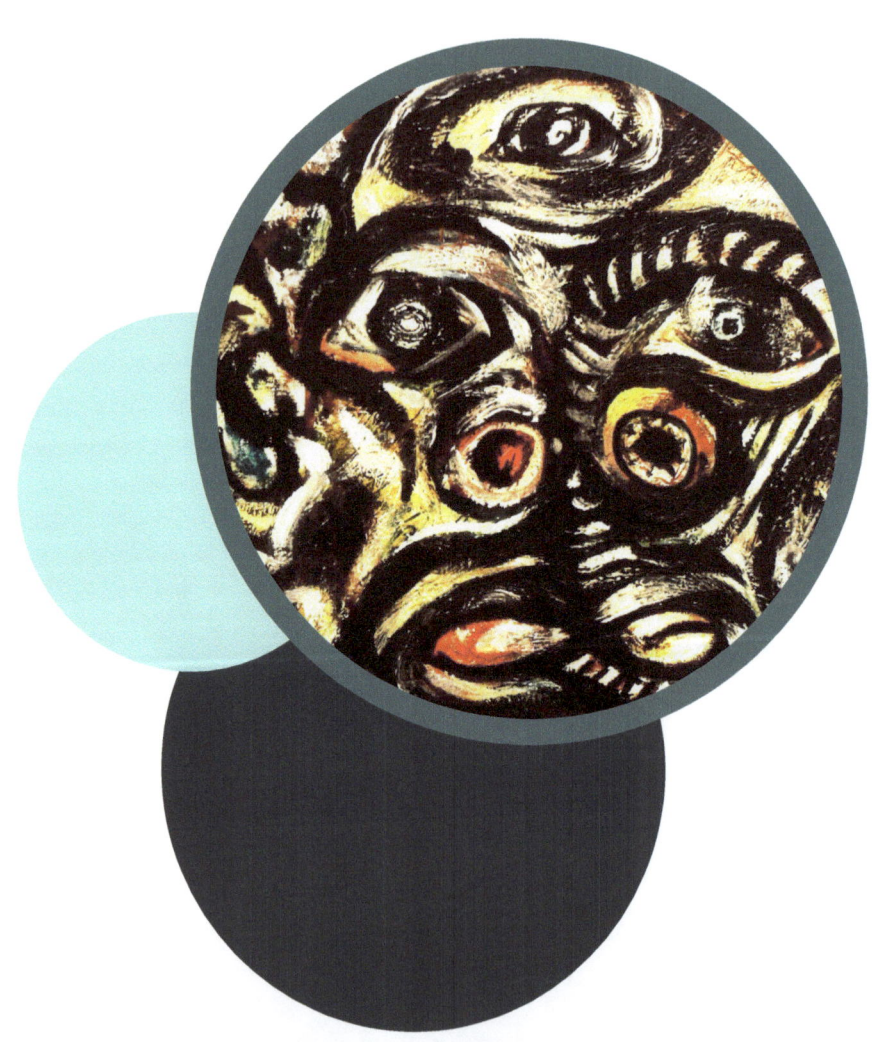

the **influencers**

By studying the work of these and other important artists, you can gain a better understanding of the unique properties and possibilities of acrylic paint, and how it has been used by artists to create a wide range of styles and techniques over the years.

Jackson Pollock
Pollock was a key figure in the development of abstract expressionism, and is known for his "drip" paintings created using acrylic paint. His use of the medium helped to popularize acrylic paint among artists.

Mark Rothko
Rothko was another prominent figure in the abstract expressionist movement, known for his large-scale color field paintings. He used acrylic paint to create his signature soft-edged shapes and rich, saturated colors.

David Hockney
Hockney is a contemporary artist who has used acrylic paint extensively in his work. His bright, bold color palette and use of flat, geometric shapes have influenced many artists working in the medium today.

Gerhard Richter
Richter is a German artist who has worked in a variety of media, including acrylic paint. His signature blurred and smeared images are created using a technique known as squeegee painting, in which layers of paint are applied and scraped away with a tool.

Helen Frankenthaler
Frankenthaler was a leading figure in the color field movement, and is known for her use of acrylic paint to create large-scale, abstract compositions. She developed a technique known as "soak-stain" painting, in which she poured diluted paint onto unprimed canvas to create a watercolor-like effect.

Anselm Kiefer
Kiefer is a German artist who has used acrylic paint extensively in his work. His large-scale, mixed media paintings often incorporate materials such as sand, straw, and lead, and explore themes of memory, history, and myth.

Jean-Michel Basquiat
Basquiat was an American artist who rose to prominence in the 1980s. His graffiti-inspired paintings often featured text and social commentary, and he used acrylic paint to create bold, expressive marks.

Alma Thomas
Thomas was an American artist who began her career as a schoolteacher before turning to painting full-time. Her abstract compositions often featured bright, swirling colors, and she used acrylic paint to create luminous, layered surfaces.

Kerry James Marshall
Marshall is an American artist known for his large-scale paintings that explore the black experience in America. His use of acrylic paint allows him to create rich, saturated colors and highly detailed compositions.

Faith Ringgold
Ringgold is an American artist known for her narrative quilts and paintings that address issues of race and gender. Her acrylic paintings often feature bright, bold colors and intricate patterns.

Jacob Lawrence
Lawrence was an American artist known for his narrative paintings that depicted the experiences of African Americans throughout history. He often used acrylic paint to create flat, colorful compositions that combined elements of folk art and modernism.

more resources

YouTube Art TIPS:
@ashmccllc

Art Supplies:
ASHMCC-Crafts

Questions?
ashley@ashmcc.net

about the **author**

I've always had a deep passion for art and painting, as well as a fascination with graphic design. I truly believe that creativity is the key to unlocking human potential and helping individuals achieve their dreams.

With years of experience in the art and design field, I'm passionate about helping others develop their craft and achieve their goals. Whether you're a beginner looking to learn the fundamentals of art and design or a seasoned pro seeking to take your career to the next level, I'm here to guide you every step of the way.

Let's unlock your creative potential together!

www.ingramcontent.com/pod-product-compliance
Lightning Source LLC
Chambersburg PA
CBHW061616230526
45473CB00031BA/2605